basketball's new wave

Chamique Holdsclaw

Driving Force

BY
MARK **S**TEWART

THE MILLBROOK PRESS
BROOKFIELD, CONNECTICUT

M

THE MILLBROOK PRESS

Produced by
BITTERSWEET PUBLISHING
John Sammis, President
and
TEAM STEWART, INC.

Series Design and Electronic Page Makeup by
JAFFE ENTERPRISES
Ron Jaffe

Researched and Edited by Mike Kennedy

All photos courtesy
AP/Wide World Photos, Inc.
except the following:
WNBA Enterprises, LLC (Mitchell Layton photographer) — Cover
Newsday — Pages 9, 11, 13, 15, 19
University of Tennessee — Pages 16, 22 bottom
Auburn University — Page 22 top
The following images are from the collection of Team Stewart:
Sports Illustrated for Kids (©1997) — Page 30
Beckett Publications, Inc. (©1999) — Page 44
Fleer/Skybox International LP (©1999) — Page 46

Printed in the United States of America

Published by
The Millbrook Press, Inc.
2 Old New Milford Road
Brookfield, Connecticut   06804

www.millbrookpress.com

Library of Congress Cataloging-in-Publication Data

Stewart, Mark.
    Chamique Holdsclaw: driving force / by Mark Stewart
    p.   cm.   — (Basketball's new wave)
    Includes bibliographical references and index.
    Summary: Profiles the life and career of Chamique Holdsclaw, star of the Washington Mystics women's
basketball team.
    ISBN 0-7613-1801-1 (lib. bdg.)
    1. Holdsclaw, Chamique—Juvenile literature. 2. Basketball players—United States—Biography—
Juvenile literature. 3. Women Basketball Players—United States—Biography—Juvenile literature.
[1. Holdsclaw, Chamique 2. Basketball players. 3. Women—Biography. 4. Afro-Americans—Biography]
I. Title. II. Series.
GV884.H63 S74 2000
796.323′092—dc21
[B]   99-087319

lib: 1 3 5 7 9 10 8 6 4 2

Contents

The Courts of Queens

chapter 1

"I want to be different from anyone, ever."
— CHAMIQUE HOLDSCLAW

The playgrounds of New York City have always held a special place in the history of basketball. Some of the game's best players and legendary innovators have come from the asphalt courts of Brooklyn, Queens, Manhattan, and the Bronx. In these gigantic hoops "laboratories," no limits are placed on creativity, talent, or ferocity. As a result, almost every day someone in the city does something no one has ever seen before. Reputations are made and broken on an hourly basis. And the games go on, rain or shine, in the searing heat or freezing cold. This is a world where fact and fiction merge into legend. It is not a place for the timid. And certainly no place for girls.

Or, at least, that was what everyone believed until a young lady named Chamique Holdsclaw came along.

As a child, she found her way to the courts of Queens in order to escape the turmoil in her home. Her parents, Willie and Bonita, were young and poorly educated, and had a difficult time finding steady work. They fought constantly and said terrible things to each other, things that upset and confused Chamique (pronounced sha-MEEK-wa) and her younger brother, Davon.

Chamique Holdsclaw had plenty to smile about when she became the WNBA's No. 1 draft pick in the spring of 1999. Growing up in New York, she knew little happiness in her home.

This New York City playground was named in honor of local legend Earl "The Goat" Manigault. It may not be long before Chamique has a court named after her.

Knowing what was in store for her when she walked through her front door, Chamique looked for any reason *not* to come straight home after school. She got involved in a number of extra-curricular activities, and sometimes just hung out with her girlfriends. As the years progressed, however, Chamique found that she needed something more.

That is when basketball became an important part of her day. It not only let her forget her troubles, but it also provided a focus for her life. Soon all it took was the sound of a bouncing ball to make Chamique drop everything and lose herself in a game. Her love for the sport became so intense that her friends in grade school nick-named her "Flat Out," because she would flat-out forget whatever she was doing if she thought she could get into a game.

The vast majority of the people Chamique played against were boys, some her own age and some older. Almost all of the people she played against were either

Did You Know?

On one youth league team for which Chamique played, her backup was Ron Artest—a first-round selection of the Chicago Bulls in the 1999 NBA Draft.

bigger or faster or stronger. To hold her own, Chamique had to use her mind as well as her body. Like a basketball computer, she developed a move for every situation, and a strategy for every opponent. "Big boys, small boys—whoever—I was always ready to take them on," she says. "I wasn't scared of anybody's game."

Chamique's greatest fear was that her parents would split up. Sometimes this made her sad, but usually it just made her frustrated and angry. Either way, she never let it show. By the age of nine, Chamique was viewed by her relatives as the most mature person in the house. "I had to make sure things didn't fall too much out of order," she remembers. "If they did, I'd call my grandmother or my aunts and uncles."

The family's financial situation grew worse and worse, and the arguing became more frequent and louder. In 1988, when Chamique was 11, the strain became too much and the family fell apart. Willie left their apartment in Astoria, Davon stayed with his mother, and Chamique decided she would be happier with her grandmother, June, who worked for a Queens hospital but lived in Manhattan. It was the right choice—from the moment she moved in, she felt more relaxed and in control. Chamique and June were truly birds of a feather. "A lot of people say, 'You act like a grandmother,'" Chamique laughs. 'You're just totally laid back—nothing bothers you.'"

With June's love and support, Chamique began to excel, both in the classroom and on the court. She enrolled at Queens Lutheran School, where she played on an organized basketball team for the first time. Playing for a coach with a set system was great for her game. Chamique sharpened her skills through drills and practice, and also began to understand how her talent could benefit others on her team.

That was when the winning started.

Three generations of Holdsclaw women: June, Bonita, and Chamique.

Flat Out Fabulous

> *"From eighth grade on, she was always a winner. She just thought it always belonged to her."*
>
> —JUNE HOLDSCLAW

You can tell a lot about basketball players when they are young. If they are long and lanky, the chances are excellent that they will continue to grow. If they are well-coordinated and possess unusual strength, it is a good bet that they will be well-coordinated and even stronger when they grow up. As an eighth grader at Queens Lutheran, Chamique Holdsclaw was all those things and much, much more.

Chamique seemed to be playing a different game at a different speed. She could shoot accurately from anywhere on the floor, and specialized at slicing through tiny openings for easy layups. On defense, she often knew what her opponents would do before they knew themselves, and was almost always in the right place at the right time.

"I've always been a step ahead," says Chamique, who believes her turbulent childhood taught her how to anticipate what others will do next. "The life I've been exposed to has let me know what step to take and how not to go back a step."

*Christ the King
coach Vincent Cannizzaro*

Queens Lutheran destroyed its opponents during Chamique's eighth-grade season, and her name soon came to the attention of the top high-school coaches in the area. They could see for themselves how good she was, and they were thrilled to find that she was just as talented and competitive as a student. Most impressed was coach Vincent Cannizzaro of Christ the King High School. He and his assistants decided they would do whatever it took to get Chamique to attend their school. Even when she told them that she wanted to go to St. John's Prep, they kept the pressure on.

Finally, they got to June Holdsclaw. She listened to what the coach had to say, and she was impressed by Christ the King's basketball program and academic reputation. She told her granddaughter that it was her choice, but also let her know that she supported Coach Cannizzaro. That was all Chamique needed to hear. A few months later, in the fall of 1991, she was the starting guard for Christ the King as the Royals set out to defend the 1991 New York City Catholic High School championship they had won the previous spring.

During her freshman year, Chamique showed great maturity on the court and helped Christ the King repeat as city champs. She seemed to know when to step up and take charge, but also when to fade into the background and play a supporting role. Her numbers in the season's last two contests (in the state tournament) were typical: 16 points and 8 rebounds in the semifinals, then 8 points, 9 rebounds, and 3 blocked shots in a 58–43 wipeout of St. Peter's in the championship game. When *USA TODAY* ran its annual ratings of the nation's best freshmen, Chamique Holdsclaw was at the top of the list.

"The game of women's basketball is becoming a big-player's game. I'm one of those players who's making women's basketball from high school to college level more competitive."
CHAMIQUE HOLDSCLAW

That summer, Chamique continued to develop her game in the city's playgrounds. No longer a skinny little girl trying to talk her way into a boy's game, she was now being recognized as the top female player in town. Often, the young men guarding her took it easy at first. But they learned fast—give Chamique an opening and she's gone!

Meanwhile, Chamique was learning a style of play that had not yet hit the world of women's basketball. It was an aggressive, high-speed game where winning earned you a stay on the court and losing meant you had to sit for an hour. At first, Chamique just tried to survive and contribute a few good passes and a basket or two. But soon she was actually controlling the pace of games. When she returned to Christ the King for the basketball season, Coach Cannizzaro could hardly believe his eyes. She was simply awesome.

With their sophomore sensation in command, the Royals dominated all year, going undefeated through the regular season and state championship tournament. The bigger the game, the better Chamique played. In the season's toughest matchup, against nationally ranked O'Connell High School, she netted 26 points despite being double- and triple-teamed. In the state title game, she led Christ the King to a 62–42 win with 22 points and 20 rebounds. The victory cemented the national high-school championship for the Royals and put Chamique—who averaged 23 points a game—at the top of every college recruiter's wish list.

Chamique goes up against St. John Vianney, a top high school from New Jersey.

Dear Diary

chapter }

"I know I'm good. But I can be that much better."

— CHAMIQUE HOLDSCLAW

To those who witnessed the remarkable rise of Chamique Holsclaw during her sophomore season, it did not seem possible for a high-school player to get much better. Yet when she returned from another summer of nonstop basketball, she was not only better but bigger and taller, too. Standing more than 6 feet (183 cm) tall, Chamique could see eye-to-eye with many of the centers that Christ the King played, yet she handled and shot the ball better than the best guards. She was always under control, always searching for a scoring opportunity, and always very, very dangerous.

Already the most celebrated high-school player in the city, Chamique gained national attention when *USA TODAY* asked her to keep a diary of her

Did You Know?

Chamique got her SAT scores back a few weeks after taking the test. She killed on the math section and did better than she expected on the English.

season. Not surprisingly, she took her writing assignment as seriously as her homework

The queen and her castle: Chamique poses in front of Christ the King.

and her hoops. "I wasn't going to be average," she says. That went for everything, not just basketball. She proved intelligent, analytical, articulate, and even witty at times.

The diary was just one of the new challenges Chamique faced during her junior year of high school. First, there was the Scholastic Aptitude Test, a combination English-and-math exam taken by college-bound juniors and seniors. How you score on the SATs goes a long way in determining which schools will accept your application. Chamique knew that her basketball would earn her a university scholarship, but she wanted to do well enough so she could get into a really good academic school. There was no women's pro basketball league in the United States at the time, so a top-notch education would be the big payoff for her years of hard work and dedication on the court. The test took place on November 6, the morning of her first basketball practice.

> "My grandmother taught me to count my blessings. There's always an upside to whatever bad happens."
>
> **CHAMIQUE HOLDSCLAW**

The excitement of the season and the pressure of the SATs nearly drove her crazy!

The college recruiters were also driving Chamique crazy. The process began in January 1994, and did not let up for nearly 10 months. At almost every game she played, there were a dozen or more college scouts in the stands; wherever she went during her junior year, she ran into someone giving a sales pitch for a school. It got to the point where Chamique was afraid to talk to anyone, including her closest friends. "It's really strange to have someone always watching you," she remembers.

The greatest challenge of all for Chamique during her junior year was reconciling with her mother. It had been nearly five years since they had last lived together, and for much of that time they did not have regular contact. Slowly but surely, as Bonita got her life together and as Chamique began to understand more about the world, mother and daughter began to reconnect. They spent Thanksgiving and Christmas together in 1993, and for the first time in her life, Chamique was able to relax when she was around her mom.

The 1993–94 basketball season started with a surprising loss for Christ the King, as the Royals dropped their opening game to Archbishop Carroll. After that, however, it was smooth sailing. Chamique, now a co-captain, took charge and led the team in scoring and rebounding. In a victory over St. John Vianney, one of New Jersey's best schools, she scored 23 points, pulled down 25 rebounds, blocked 7 shots, and led a miracle comeback that saw Christ the King erase a 7-point deficit in the final two minutes. That same week, Chamique aced her midterm exams in art, religion, and math.

Chamique controls the action during the 1994 league championship game.

By the end of the season, it seemed as if Chamique's name was in the papers every other day. In the space of a few weeks, she scored her 1,000th point, made several different prep All-America teams, and was named New York's high-school Player of the Year. Christ the King, meanwhile, rolled to league, city, and state championships for the third consecutive year.

After the season, Chamique turned her attention to choosing a college. In her mind, she had narrowed down the possibilities to a dozen or so top schools. Chamique's "short list" heading into the summer consisted of Tennessee, Purdue, Virginia, and Connecticut, but she kept her mind open. It was not until October 1994—just prior to her senior season—that she finally made up her mind. Despite promises from dozens of excellent schools that she would be treated like a queen and transformed into a national star, Chamique selected the University of Tennessee. The weekend she spent on the Knoxville campus that fall had opened her eyes. The only guarantee made by coach Pat Summitt was that she would drive her harder than she had ever been driven, and that she would get only as much playing time as she earned. And she wouldn't even get a *uniform* if she did not keep up with her studies. To Chamique, that sounded like the kind challenge she was looking for.

In her mind, Chamique believed she could step right into the Lady Vols' starting lineup as a freshman. But she also knew that, if she did not, it would be because there were better players in front of her. As she saw it, that meant Tennessee would have one heck of a team—and a clear shot at the ultimate goal in women's basketball during the mid-1990s: the national championship.

During the recruiting process, Chamique had impressed Coach Summitt as a serious and dedicated young lady. But it was important to let Summitt know she had a "lighter" side. This she demonstrated by calling her future coach and practically giving her a heart attack. "I said, 'Coach Summitt, I've made my decision—I'm going to the University of Virginia.'"

"Then I said, '*Psych*—I'm coming to Tennessee!'"

Tennessee coach Pat Summitt impressed Chamique with her no-nonsense approach.

Free and Clear

chapter **4**

"If ever a kid could consider
herself a superstar and act
like she's above everybody, she
certainly could. But she never has."

— COACH CANNIZZARO

Free of annoying recruiters and clear about her future plans, Chamique Holdsclaw turned in what has to be one of the greatest senior seasons in the history of high-school hoops. In Christ the King's opener, she poured in 30 points and added 11 rebounds and 7 blocked shots as the Royals demolished Altoona High, the fourth-ranked team in the country.

Most teams that faced Chamique during her senior season left the court feeling as if they had just been hit by a bus. Christ the King pounded one opponent after another. And although Chamique usually did most of the damage, her teammates became quite adept at finishing off a wounded enemy. As the year progressed, it became obvious that Christ the King was on its way to an undefeated season. They were beating the top teams in the city, and traveling to tournaments outside New York to trounce the best teams in the region. It was also clear that Chamique had taught her teammates how

> "My teammates know I'm down to earth. I'll joke with them. But when it comes to basketball, I try to be serious about it."
> **CHAMIQUE HOLDSCLAW**

to win without her. Many believed that the Royals would be even stronger *after* she graduated!

Perhaps that is why the New York City Catholic High School Athletic Association met in February 1995. The topic of discussion was rules violations that league members might have committed. The result of the meeting was a ruling that Christ the King had broken a new rule limiting the number of out-of-state trips a school could make. It was a minor violation, but it had major consequences: The Royals were suspended for the remainder of their league schedule. Chamique and her teammates were devastated; school officials were livid. They claimed that their school was being punished for being too good.

The issue went before the courts, and fortunately Christ the King won in time to get back on the court for the league tournament. The Royals rolled through the play-offs to take another Catholic Schools title, then moved on to the state championship, where they defeated Sachem in the final. Chamique finished the final year of her prep career averaging 25 points, 15 rebounds, 5 blocks, 3 assists, and 4 steals per game. She also was named national Player of the Year.

During Chamique's time at Christ the King, the varsity basketball team lost just four of the 110 games it played. She graduated as the school's all-time scorer and rebounder, and became the only player, male or female, to be voted

The trophy case at Christ the King before Chamique graduated. It is a bit more crowded now.

New York City's Player of the Year for three straight seasons. Some sportswriters were already predicting she would one day take the women's game to a new level, and were quick to point out that she shared uniform number 23 with Michael Jordan, who had ushered in a new era in men's basketball.

This kind of talk easily can go to a young person's head. And no one would have blamed Chamique if she had developed a little bit of an attitude. But that was never the case. Grandma June had always taught her to be modest and respectful. Also, Chamique knew that her skills and intelligence would face far greater tests in the years to come, as the competition got better and the stakes became higher. Acting high and mighty at this point would have made her feel foolish.

A talented inside player, Chamique could outjump and outmuscle bigger opponents when she needed to.

A Million Miles Away

chapter

"I can leave my door unlocked and everything's still there when I get back."
— CHAMIQUE HOLDSCLAW

Everyone who moves far from home to attend college goes through a period of adjustment—a little homesickness, a little confusion, a little anxiety. Chamique's adjustment lasted about as long as it took to unpack. When she opened the door and stepped into her dorm room at Tennessee, it was as if she had entered an entirely new universe. People were nice, the pace of life was easy, and she no longer sensed the hint of danger that always seemed to hang in the air back in New York. Chamique signed up for classes, got to know her way around the UT campus, and started making friends.

When basketball practice began, she started turning heads. The UT staff had heard from Chamique's high-school coaches that she always came back from the summer with a new wrinkle in her game. Pat Summitt had penciled Chamique into the role of a slashing, penetrating forward who could pop off the bench and create matchup problems for opponents. But in preparation for her college career, Chamique had honed her long-range jumper and become a deadly outside shooter. Coach Summitt knew instantly that this was no ordinary freshman. So she decided she would not treat Chamique like one.

Chamique turns the corner and runs defender Lisa Ostrom into a teammate's pick in a 1998 game against Vanderbilt. When Chamique arrived at UT in 1995, she was not as confident about taking the ball to the basket.

> "I've never seen a freshman come in and play with such confidence and poise. She's a leader."
> AUBURN COACH JOE CIAMPI

Instead, Summitt picked out the one flaw in Chamique's game—her first step—and drove her relentlessly to improve. It was not that Chamique was slow, it was that she could be quicker. Because the college game is much faster than high-school basketball, Chamique did not improve instantly. This was a shock to her; in the past, she usually got better at something as soon as she set her mind to it. After a couple of weeks, with all the criticism from the coaches and her own mounting frustration, Chamique started to get down on herself for the first time in her life. She was a perfectionist, and suddenly she was no longer perfect.

One poor workout followed another until a few words from teammate Abby Conklin helped to snap her out of it. "Once after a bad practice she told me, 'You're an awesome player,'" Chamique remembers. "'But you're not showing your talent.'" Chamique knew she was right. If she just relaxed and played her game, the improvement would come.

Soon Chamique was playing with confidence again. That was bad news for the U.S. Olympic team, which had scheduled a stop in Knoxville for a "tune-up" exhibition against the Lady Vols. They got tuned up all right; in fact, they nearly got overhauled. The freshman shredded Team USA at both ends of the court, scoring 19 points against the top women in the world. This began a four-year love affair between UT fans and their

Thompson-Boling Arena

young star. From that day forward, every time Chamique's name was announced, the Tennessee faithful rocked the roof of Thompson-Boling Arena.

After eight games, the Lady Vols had a perfect record and were ranked second in the country. Chamique played the starring role in most of those victories, leading the team in scoring and rebounding. In her first month, she established new school records for points (27) and rebounds (16) by a freshman. Naturally, her teammates began looking to her when they needed a big shot, but Chamique did not yet feel comfortable in that role. She preferred to let the more experienced players take command down the stretch, despite Coach Summitt's instructions to step up and take charge when the game was on the line.

The Holdsclaw File

CHAMIQUE'S FAVORITE...

Magazine . . . . SLAM

Cable Channel . . . . Nickelodeon

Athlete . . . . Michael Jordan

Historical Figures . . Marcus Garvey and Martin Luther King, Jr.

Chamique does not wear number 23 because it was Michael Jordan's number. Deeply religious, her favorite part of the Bible is Psalm 23.

Chamique's reluctance to assert herself began to hurt the Lady Vols. In January, against the defending champs from the University of Connecticut, she "disappeared" in the final minutes, scoring just one basket. On several occasions, Chamique passed up chances to take the game to the Huskies, playing tentatively instead. UConn won the game, becoming the first opponent to win on Tennessee's home floor in four seasons. "I made kind of a freshman mistake," she says. "My nature is not to be a pushy person. And I kind of watched there when we fell behind, thinking the upperclassmen would help us come back, instead of getting in there myself. I was like a spectator when I should have been doing all I could."

Fortunately for UT, Chamique is not someone who makes the same mistake twice. She immediately redeemed herself against heavily favored Louisiana Tech, scoring 23 points and hauling down 13 rebounds. Leon Barmore, head coach of the Lady Techsters, did everything he could to shut down Chamique, but she had an answer for every tactic his players tried. Barmore later said that Chamique had greatness written upon her.

The victory over Louisiana Tech ignited the Lady Vols. They continued to beat nationally ranked opponents and stormed into the Southeast Conference (SEC) tournament as big favorites. Nine minutes into the championship game, however, the unthinkable occurred. Chamique fell to the floor, clutching her right knee. She sat out the rest of the game and cheered on her teammates, as they rallied to defeat Alabama. But the news in the locker room afterward was not good. Chamique had suffered a slight tear to a ligament in her knee.

Did You Know?

After their 1996 NCAA championship, the Lady Vols were invited to Washington, DC, where they were congratulated by the Clintons at a White House ceremony.

With a dozen days until the opening game of her very first NCAA Tournament, Chamique began a grueling rehabilitation program. She strengthened the damaged knee and wore a brace to protect it from further injury. She was back on the floor in time for the NCAAs, and was a big contributor as the Lady Vols fought their way to a berth in the Final Four.

Now, just two wins separated Tennessee from the national championship. The team's first opponent was Connecticut. Hoping to redeem herself for her poor showing in January, Chamique tried a bit too hard and forced too many shots. She made up for her inconsistent shooting with good passing and defense, and the Lady Vols held on to win. In the championship game, Tennessee faced SEC rival Georgia. In the locker room, Chamique assured her teammates she was ready to play, and reminded them that the team that defended better would win. She even scrawled "Defense Wins Championships" on her sneakers to drive home the point. Chamique scored 16 and grabbed 14 rebounds against Georgia. True to her word, Tennessee's stifling defense proved to be the difference in an 83–65 victory.

The Lady Vols were treated to a thunderous welcome when they returned to campus. For Chamique, it was the fulfillment of a lifelong dream and, at the same time, just "another day at the office." Incredibly, every spring, since eighth grade, she had ended the year as a champion.

The Lady Vols celebrate their 1996 national championship.
Michelle Marciniak holds the team's trophy aloft.

Leading Lady

chapter 6

> *"I know that I have been blessed with a lot of talent. I just need to bring that talent into a team concept."*
>
> — CHAMIQUE HOLDSCLAW

Pat Summitt is not the kind of basketball coach who will sit quietly and watch her players self-destruct. Still, years of experience have taught her that the best way for a team to come together is for a leader to emerge. As the 1996–97 season began, Coach Summitt knew that it was only a matter of time until Chamique stepped forward and filled this role. Unfortunately, time was not on the Lady Vols' side. After 16 games, their record stood at just 10–6. And the toughest part of their schedule still lay ahead.

In women's basketball, team leaders generally play the guard position. Their passes and play-calling trigger the offense, and they apply relentless pressure on defense. The starting guards from Tennessee's 1996 championship squad had graduated, leaving backcourt duties to inexperienced newcomers. Though a forward—and just a sophomore—Chamique was the obvious choice to take control.

Chamique was playing great basketball, scoring points in bunches and averaging nearly 10 rebounds a game. She netted her 1,000th career point faster than any player in school history. But it was not until January, during a closed-door meeting, that she finally became the team's true leader. Chamique tore into her teammates for their inconsistent performances, and she reminded them how they had won the year before. When the game is on the line, the team that digs deepest and finds a little extra intensity is usually the one that wins. Now the whole *season* was on the line, Chamique said, and it was time for Tennessee to defend its championship. And they would start with the thing that had gotten them to the Final Four a year earlier: defense.

"They weren't getting the job done," she says of her decision to speak out. As the next few weeks proved, her decision was a smart one. The Lady Vols finished their season with a flourish, winning 11 of 12 games. They played with great intensity, wearing down opponents for 30 minutes and then putting them away in the final 10. Chamique's efforts on defense were magnificent. In a game against Wisconsin–Green Bay, she racked up seven steals.

Pat Summitt spurs her players to victory during the 1997 NCAA Tournament. The underdog Lady Vols surprised everyone by repeating as national champions.

Thanks to their late-season surge, the Lady Vols made it back to the NCAA Tournament. No one except Coach Summitt and her players believed they had a chance. Tennessee came into the big event with 10 losses, and no team with so many defeats had ever won the championship. UT did not even finish first in its own

Chamique leaps into Abby Conklin's arms after the final buzzer sounds on UT's marvelous upset of the UConn Huskies in 1997.

conference—in fact, the Lady Vols came in fifth in the SEC! Chamique and her teammates saw it differently. They had played the nation's toughest schedule, so naturally they were now the nation's toughest team.

Tennessee made quick work of its early-round opponents, defeating Grambling and Oregon by big scores. Against Colorado, the underdog Lady Vols scored an eight-point victory to set up a showdown with UConn. The Huskies had spent the entire season at the top of the national rankings, and were undefeated in 33 games. One of those wins was an embarrassing 15-point blowout of the Lady Vols.

The UConn game was a classic. Tennessee did everything right, but UConn's talent kept the score close. Not until the final moments did UT pull away for a victory. The Connecticut players could not believe they lost. Indeed, it was the biggest upset of the season.

Summitt
Conference

Tennessee coach Pat Summitt rarely minces words when asked about Chamique Holdsclaw. Here are some of the things she has said about her superstar:

"The more pressure there is, the more desire she has to make plays."

"When you have a player like Chamique, you appear a lot smarter, a lot better under pressure, and you win a lot more."

"She's had a lot to deal with, with the spotlight on her all the time. She's still quiet and shy and very soft-spoken, but she's more self-assured than ever before."

"It's amazing how graceful, fluid, and efficient she is. Sometimes, Chamique makes it look so easy."

"I would not trade Chamique for any player in the country."

"She's the best I ever coached."

Beth Morgan (left) can only watch as Chamique glides to the hoop for two of her 31 points against Notre Dame in the 1997 national semifinal.

Now the Lady Vols were on a roll. They did not care who they had to play or what their record was—they were going to find a way to win the championship. In the semifinals they faced Notre Dame, another team that had heated up just in time for the tournament. Tennessee defenders swarmed all over Notre Dame star Beth Morgan, forcing her to miss 15 shots. Chamique, meanwhile, scored 31 points and had 4 steals. After the game, Abby Conklin was asked by reporters where the Lady Vols would be without Chamique Holdsclaw. "Spring break," she answered.

The NCAA Final brought Tennessee face-to-face with another powerhouse team, Old Dominion University. Like UConn, ODU came into the game with a 33-game winning streak. But twice during the tournament opponents had taken the Lady Monarchs to overtime before losing. Though still the favorite, Old Dominion was far from invincible.

The two teams traded blows in the early going, then it appeared as if Tennessee was ready to deliver the knockout punch. Behind Chamique's brilliant play, they surged to a

Chamique was just a sophomore when her first trading card came out.

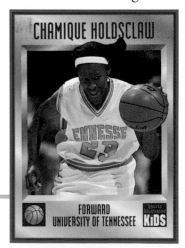

CHAMIQUE HOLDSCLAW

FORWARD
UNIVERSITY OF TENNESSEE

16-point lead. But the Lady Monarchs clawed back, eventually regaining the lead at 49–47 with seven minutes left. It was panic time in the Tennessee huddle; the game was about to slip away. Coach Summitt and her star player exchanged glances. Chamique knew that it was on her shoulders now.

Over the next few minutes, Chamique sank three tough shots and set up teammates for two more. The final hoop gave UT an eight-point lead, and they held on until the final buzzer for a 68–59 victory. Chamique was named the tournament's Most Outstanding Player. Many of those in attendance that day felt that was not enough. They were saying she might be the best player ever in women's basketball.

Chamique takes it right to Old Dominion's Nyree Roberts during the 1997 NCAA Final.

Stepping Up

"I want to become one of the best players that ever played the game and hopefully win as many national championships as I possibly can."

— CHAMIQUE HOLDSCLAW

The summer of 1997 saw Chamique Holdsclaw in a familiar situation. Just as she had every year since grade school, she spent the break looking for the best game available. Only this time, she found it. She was invited to join Team USA for a 12-game tour of Canada and Europe. The only college player on the squad, Chamique looked forward to learning some new tricks from the old pros. She was also anxious to see how she compared to players with experience in the newly formed women's pro leagues, the ABL and WNBA.

At the end of the tour, Chamique was Team USA's leading scorer and rebounder. A month later, she was invited to join Team USA in the qualifying rounds for the World Championships of Basketball. This time, the squad flew down to Brazil. And once again, Chamique was nothing short of sensational. She hit 7 of every 10 shots from the

Me and T

During Team USA's summer tour in 1997, Chamique roomed with 33-year-old Teresa Edwards, a veteran of four Olympics and coach of the ABL's Atlanta Glory. T and Chamique talked for endless hours about the finer points of the game; the young star came out of the experience with an entirely new perspective on basketball. "I was under her influence, learning," recalls Chamique. "She's the ultimate player. I was trying to feel how she looks at the game. As a player, you like to see how others look at basketball, what decisions they make."

The most important thing Chamique learned was that defense can produce offense. When every defender gives an all-out effort to trap and smother the ball, it often results in the kind of turnover that leads to an easy, uncontested layup. Chamique returned to Tennessee for her junior season and dedicated herself to becoming a superior "end-to-end" per-former. "On the national team," she says, "I learned that not only do I have to be a scorer, but also a passer and a defender."

Nikki McCray and Chamique celebrate a Team USA victory. Years later, they would be teammates in the pros.

field and 9 of every 10 from the free throw line. She celebrated her 20th birthday in style, with 32 points against Cuba.

When Chamique got back to campus, she found herself besieged by the media. It seemed as if every newspaper, magazine, TV and radio station within 1,000 miles wanted to interview her. And they all had the same question: Are you turning pro?

Turning pro? Chamique was mystified. Yes, playing pro ball was in her plans, but why in the world would she throw away an education to make a few dollars in the ABL or WNBA? Besides, didn't both leagues have strict rules about signing players before they graduated? As Chamique soon found out, she did not have the complete picture.

Chamique was a hot property. So hot, some claimed, that the two pro leagues would probably be willing to bend a lot of rules to sign her. Whichever league got her stood a good chance of sinking its rival, so they would find ways to pay her that did not interfere with salary caps or other regulations. And as for her degree, well, surely someone would think of a clever way around that. In short, if Chamique wanted to play, she could make millions right away. For a girl who had seen firsthand how money problems can tear a family apart, the lure of the pros must have been strong.

Chamique decided to stay put. In fact, her thoughts were quite clear on the matter. "God forbid we don't win the championship," she says of her decision to stay for her final two years. "I'd want to come back and work for that third one. If we do win, I'm going to want that fourth one."

Winning a third consecutive national championship was not out of the question. In fact, the Lady Vols went into the season favored to repeat. The miracle team of 1996–97 was now battle-tested, while the incoming freshman class featured three top recruits: Ace Clement, Semeka Randall, and 1997 High School Player of the Year Tamika Catchings, the daughter of former NBA player Harvey Catchings.

The biggest difference in the team, however, was Chamique. She was in the best shape of her life, and her success on the international level had her brimming with confidence. Chamique also had a firmer grasp on her position as team leader. Never much of a "rah-rah" person, she decided instead to lead by example. So while other players took water breaks in practice, she would go shoot extra free throws. When her teammates were changing, she would watch a half-hour of game films.

Coach Summitt had little to fret about during the 1997–98 season. Game after game, the team made the key plays when it needed to, scoring important baskets, getting big rebounds, and making defensive stops when opponents got close. The freshmen blended into the lineup beautifully, with Catchings and Randall playing major roles in the team's success. Along with Chamique, they formed the "Three Meeks."

Chamique was a cool, confident team leader during the 1997–98 season, when UT went undefeated.

Two of the "Three Meeks"—Chamique and Semeka Randall—celebrate a win over UNC during the 1998 NCAA Tournament.

The Lady Vols were playing perfect basketball, and their record reflected it. Heading into the NCAA Tournament, they had not lost once in 33 games. The road to a third straight title was equally smooth, as UT trounced its first three opponents by an average of 35 points, then edged North Carolina by six to make the Final Four. In the national semifinal Tennessee destroyed Arkansas, 86–58. In the NCAA Final, it was more of the same, as the Lady Vols polished off Louisiana Tech with ease. Chamique saw right away that Tech could not stop her, and decided to pour it on early and often. In the first six minutes, she scored a dozen points to give Tennessee a 21–8 lead. By halftime, Chamique had 18 points, 7 rebounds, and 5 assists to put the Lady Vols up by 22. The second half was little more than a basketball clinic, as UT stuffed every attempt the Bulldogs made to get back in the game. When the final buzzer sounded Tennessee was a 93–75 winner, and Chamique was a no-brainer for the tournament's Most Outstanding Player award. "It was women's basketball at an entirely new level," she says of the team's performance.

Did You Know?

Tennessee's 39-0 season in 1997-98 ranks as the best record by any team—male or female, at any level—in the history of NCAA basketball.

Chamique shows off her third NCAA championship trophy. The decision to stay at UT for another year was easy, she says. "The only way I'd have come out is if Coach Summitt told me to."

Better and Better

chapter **8**

"She has taken her game to another level, and I wasn't sure she was capable of doing that."

— PAT SUMMITT

A few weeks after winning her third NCAA title and second Player of the Year award, Chamique pulled on her Team USA uniform and traveled to Berlin, Germany, for the World Championships of Basketball. A year earlier, she had been a wide-eyed rookie getting a first taste of international competition. Now Chamique was devouring her opponents. Team USA rolled to a 9–0 record and took the gold medal.

Chamique accepts the Associated Press Player of the Year trophy in the spring of 1999.

Chamique (back row) poses with members of the 1999 Kodak All-America Team. Her Tennessee teammates, Tamika Catchings and Semeka Randall, made the squad, too.

Chamique returned to Tennessee for her senior season stronger, faster, and more focused than ever on playing great basketball. Even Coach Summitt was a little surprised how good her star player had become. She knew by now not to put a ceiling on Chamique's talent and determination, but it was pretty awesome to think that the best player in the college game could just keep getting better and better.

Chamique cries on Coach Summitt's shoulder in the closing moments of UT's 69–63 loss to Duke in the 1999 NCAA Tournament.

Even so, the challenges that lay ahead figured to be significant. Every opponent would be looking to make her reputation against Chamique, and each enemy coach would be plotting a way to derail UT in its run for a fourth straight championship. Off the court, Chamique would have to deal with an insane media blitz. Thousands of requests for interviews and photo shoots poured in, and despite declining most, she would still end up doing close to 700. On game days, Chamique needed a police escort to get from her dorm to the arena. And after games, she had to sit in a special area, where she signed hundreds of autographs.

Through all the commotion, Chamique played spectacular basketball. An early-season loss to Purdue served as a wakeup call for the Lady Vols, who turned it up a notch and roared through the rest of their season. As Chamique poured in points, the personal honors poured. She was named a First-Team All-American for the fourth time, Player of the Year for a third time, and was voted to Kodak's 25th Anniversary all-time All-America squad. Chamique also won the Sullivan Award as the nation's top amateur athlete—the only time a women's basketball player ever won the

college *stats*

Season	Games	Assists/Game	Rebounds/Game	Points/Game
1995–96	36	2.1	9.1	16.2
1996–97	39	2.9	9.4	20.6
1997–98	39	3.0	8.4	23.5
1998–99	34	2.4	8.1	21.3
Total	148	2.6	8.8	20.4

college *achievements*

NCAA Rookie of the Year 1996
NCAA Champion 1996, 1997, 1998
USA Basketball Player of the Year 1997
First Team All-American 1996, 1997, 1998, 1999
Broderick Cup Winner 1998
Sullivan Award Winner 1998
NCAA Player of the Year 1997, 1998, 1999
All-Time Tennessee Scoring & Rebounding Leader
All-Time NCAA Tournament Scoring & Rebounding Leader

award. "It's a reflection of the great teammates and coaches I had," she says of the Sullivan. "It's as much their award as it is mine."

Unfortunately, Chamique's storybook college career did not have a happy ending. In the 1999 NCAA Tournament, against a smart, scrappy Duke team, Tennessee found itself in a rare struggle for survival. As always, the team looked for Chamique to take charge, but this was not her night. Duke squeezed out a 69–63 win to eliminate the Lady Vols. Chamique made just two of 18 shots and fouled out late in the second half. She left the floor in tears, shattered by the unexpected defeat.

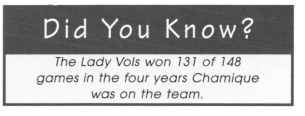

Did You Know?

The Lady Vols won 131 of 148 games in the four years Chamique was on the team.

There were a lot of tears shed for Chamique, too. College basketball fans knew they would never see a player like her again.

Meek Mania

chapter **9**

"I'm kind of glad I didn't go to New York because I don't know if I could handle all the pressure and friends and fans."

— CHAMIQUE HOLDSCLAW

Since its creation in 1997, the WNBA had viewed Chamique Holdsclaw as a key to its long-term success. For the pro game to thrive, the league believed, it would have to develop its own "personality," or trademark style of play. The first step in that process was to find a player exciting enough to get fans hooked on women's basketball. In this respect, Chamique was more than they could have hoped for. "Meek mania" began almost immediately, with WNBA President Valerie Ackerman saying she could be to the WNBA what Michael Jordan was for the NBA.

Chamique understands that the league must market her to the fans, but has her own views on

"She has done everything with class and grace, and to me, that is what stands out and gives a person staying power beyond their accomplishments on the court."

JACKIE JOYNER-KERSEE

this topic. "It's an honor to be considered in the same breath, but I'm not Michael Jordan," she says. "I'm the first Chamique Holdsclaw. And I think that's where the women's game has to get to, when women are recognized on their own."

In addition to Chamique's arrival, there was more good news for the WNBA. Prior to the 1999 season, the league expanded to 12 teams. Normally, this kind of growth would water down the quality of play. But financial struggles

Chamique is congratulated by Washington coach Nancy Darsch at the team's May 7 news conference. The Mystics general manager, NBA Hall of Famer Wes Unseld, looks on.

had caused the rival ABL to go out of business. That meant there would be dozens of proven pros available in the draft.

Thanks to their dreadful 3–27 record in 1998, the Washington Mystics owned the top pick in the 1999 draft. On May 4, they announced officially what the world had known for months: They wanted Chamique. Prior to the draft, it was assumed that a trade would be made with the New York Liberty. It would have enabled Chamique to play in her hometown, which also happens to be the WNBA's largest market. But that is not how the league and its new star player were thinking.

For a new sports league to flourish, its smaller cities must develop strong followings, and that only happens if fans feel their club can compete. Despite its poor team, Washington had supported its team loyally in 1998. That impressed Chamique. "I didn't care about their record," she says. "What I noticed is that they have such great fans. Just think of what kind of support we'll get if we're winning!"

In no time at all, Chamique became the hottest autograph in pro basketball.

"And Washington is where my grandmother wanted me to play," Chamique adds.

The fans in D.C. were so thrilled to have Chamique on their team that they staged a huge rally to welcome her the day after the draft. No one told them that their superstar rookie had to fly back to Knoxville to take her English and Psychology exams! The reception was rescheduled for May 7, and Chamique was truly touched that so many fans turned out after she had stood them up two days earlier. She knew the Mystics' fans expected the world from her, and spent her time on the podium trying to convince them to be patient. After all, she wasn't Superman.

Well, that's not what her teammates said. Speaking with reporters after the Mystics' first workout, they practically made her sound like a superhero. One player said she had never seen anyone so quick or so smooth. Another said she thought Chamique was going to dunk. And everyone was talking about her explosive first step. Mystics coach Nancy Darsch warned fans to be patient. Yes, Chamique was a great player, but she had yet to test herself over the long pro season. Every veteran in the league, said Darsch, would be "looking to teach her a thing or two."

In July 1999, Chamique became the first woman in 108 issues to grace the cover of BECKETT BASKETBALL CARD MONTHLY.

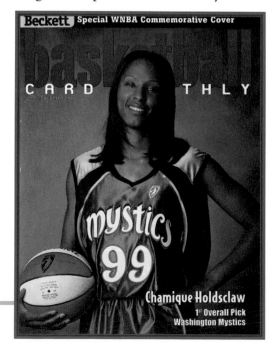

Beckett **Special WNBA Commemorative Cover**

CARD MONTHLY

mystics 99

Chamique Holdsclaw
1st Overall Pick
Washington Mystics

chapter 10 Turn the Beat Around

> *"Meek is fun to watch. She'll definitely take women's sports to a new high."*
>
> —MICHAEL JORDAN

The lessons began almost immediately. The Mystics faced the Charlotte Sting in the season opener, and their star guard, Dawn Staley, ran Chamique and her teammates ragged in an 83–73 win. Next came a thrashing at the hands of Sheryl Swoopes and Cynthia Cooper, as the defending champion Houston Comets beat Washington soundly. Chamique knew she would have to adjust to losing in the pros, but the reality of it was hard to handle.

The Mystics did not have a bad team, it just was not very "deep." Nikki McCray was a great shooter, and Shalonda Enis had been Rookie of the Year back in the ABL. But the Mystics did not have a good player in the middle, and that meant everyone had to bang around inside and help get rebounds. At the end of most games, the Mystics were too tired to stay with other teams. Finally, in front of Chamique's friends and family at New York's

"She will become a dominant player in time."
WASHINGTON MYSTICS COACH NANCY DARSCH

Chamique got her old number, 23, when she joined the Mystics. She had to "buy it" from teammate Rita Williams—it cost her a new set of golf clubs and golf lessons, too.

Madison Square Garden, the Mystics broke through for their first win of the season. Chamique scored 20 points and grabbed 9 rebounds in an 83–61 blowout. "We didn't expect to beat such a great team," she remembers, "especially such a strong defensive team. It was great to get that first win."

The Mystics returned to their losing ways in the weeks that followed, but there were signs of a turnaround. The games were closer, the losses not so lopsided, and the victories were coming more often. By August, the Mystics were within striking range of a playoff spot. They had even survived an injury to their star. In the first WNBA All-Star Game, Chamique fractured a finger. While she waited for her shooting touch to return, she concentrated on rebounding and inside scoring. As a result, she finished the year among the league's top scorers and rebounders. "I'm a confident player," she explains of her play in the paint. "I know I can score. But I'm a team player. I believe we have to go inside first."

The Mystics finished nine wins better than they had in 1998, but still missed the playoffs by three games. Chamique watched as veteran Cynthia Cooper lifted the Houston Comets to a third consecutive WNBA crown. Three championships in a row? Chamique knows how great that feels. It is something she hopes to do again as a pro.

When you watch Chamique Holdsclaw, never forget that you are witnessing history in the making. Years from now, when the story of women's basketball is written, it will closely mirror her successes, her failures, and the twists and turns in what should be a long and glorious career. Whether she likes it or not, Chamique represents the future of the pro

Chamique's 1999 cards were among the hottest in the hobby during her rookie season.

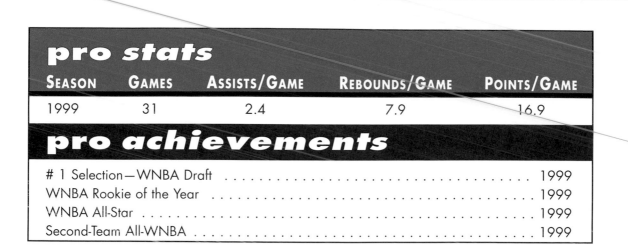

pro *stats*

SEASON	GAMES	ASSISTS/GAME	REBOUNDS/GAME	POINTS/GAME
1999	31	2.4	7.9	16.9

pro *achievements*

# 1 Selection—WNBA Draft	1999
WNBA Rookie of the Year	1999
WNBA All-Star	1999
Second-Team All-WNBA	1999

game. And by the way, she doesn't really like it. "I think it's unfair for everyone to expect me to carry the weight of the league," she says. "I need time to grow. I'm sure there are great things ahead of me. I may come out of some games and make people go, 'Wow,' then there may be other games where I might struggle. I'm just asking, 'Give me some time.'"

Being called the game's top player makes Chamique uncomfortable, too. But at least she is willing to talk about her talents, and what makes her want to keep improving. "I don't know if I'm the best," she says. "There are better shooters, better defenders, but there aren't too many females who play the game like I do. The one thing I've always done is work hard. That's not going to change. I'm not a trash-talking hotshot. I don't put myself on a pedestal. I just like to win basketball games. That's what motivates me."

Chamique chats with teammate Nikki McCray prior to the first WNBA All-Star Game.

Index